A ROAD
DOWN
IN THE
SEA

THOMAS Y. CROWELL COMPANY · NEW YORK

LORENZ GRAHAM

A ROAD DOWN IN THE SEA

PICTURES BY
GREGORIO PRESTOPINO

By the Author:

Every Man Heart Lay Down
A Road down in the Sea

Designed by *Carole Fern Halpert*

Manufactured in the United States of America

L.C. Card 74-113854   ISBN 0-690-70500-X

Library Edition 0-690-70501-8

1 2 3 4 5 6 7 8 9 10

These little poems...are told here in the words and thought patterns of a modern African boy who does not use the conventional words and phrases which by long usage often obscure the meaning of these tales in the minds of Europeans and Americans.

This is the stuff of which literature is made....

—W. E. B. Du Bois

From the Foreword of *How God Fix Jonah*, the original collection of stories from the Bible retold by Lorenz Graham, in which *A Road down in the Sea* first appeared.

Introduction

The familiar Bible stories of kings and slaves, of strength and weakness, of love and hate, were brought to Africa by missionaries. As they were retold by Africans, they took on the imagery of the people. Shepherd David with his harp of many strings, strong man Samson who was weak for woman palaver, and baby Jesus born in the place where cattle sleep are now part of the folklore of the country. To the African storyteller the Bible tale becomes a poem, or rather a spoken song. His words are simple and rhythmic. The song is sung, and it is sweet.

It was in Liberia that I first heard many of these tales, recounted in the idiom of Africans newly come to English speech.

They can be heard in many other parts of the continent as well—in the west and even in the east, wherever the English settlers spread their language.

Words of Spanish and Portuguese still remain on the African coast. "Palaver" now means something more than *palabra* ("word"). It can mean business or discussion or trouble. When "war palaver catch the country," people must fight and some must die; and "woman palaver" often lands a man in jail. "Pican" for baby or son or child comes from *pequeño* ("small") and *niño* ("child"). The two words flowed together in English speech to become first "picaninny" and then "pican."

Read again an old story. Behold a new vision with sharper images. Sway with the rhythm of the storyteller. Feel the beat of the drums.

> Long time past
> Before you papa live
> Before him papa live
> Before him pa's papa live—
>
> Long time past
> Before them big tree live
> Before them big tree's papa live—
> That time God live.

*To my father and mother
who also loved to listen to
the African storytellers.*

The Egypt people hold the Hebrews tight
And make them slaves
And make them work the farm
And work the road
And work some kind of hard.
The Hebrews cry
And sometimes they fall down and die
And all the time they moan and pray
And say "How long, O God, how long?"

God see the thing.
He hear Him people pray
And so He raise up Moses and He say
    "Moses,
    You the one
    To go fore Old King Pharoah.
    You the one to carry him My Word.
    Tell King Pharoah that I say
    'Let My people go!'
    Tell him,
    'Let My people go!' "

King Pharoah no want hear that Word
But God put Him hand there
And take the Hebrews out.
He take them all,
The mens, the womens,
The old ones and the young.
He take them out from Egypt land
He start them back to Canaan
And Moses be they leader.

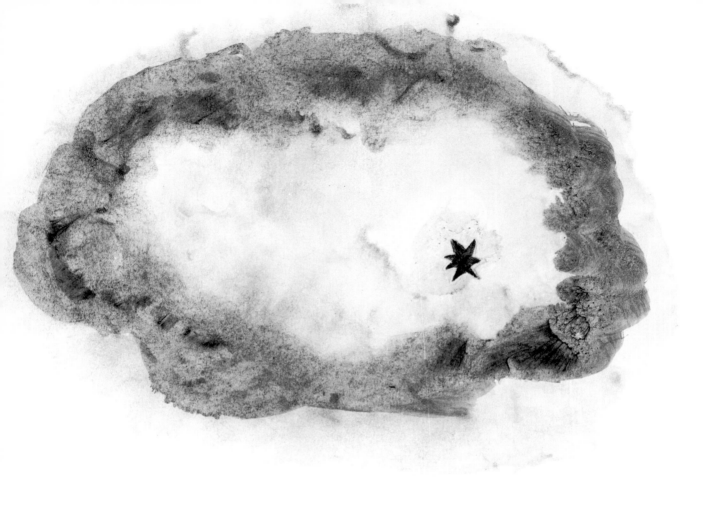

Now Moses never see that side before
And he don't know the way.

God say
　"Moses,
　Nev mind.
　I set My mark up in the sky
　You walk the way I show.
　By day My mark be in a cloud
　By night it be in fire."

And so they follow day by day
Across the sea of sand
And on the mountains
And in bush and swamp.

And they be plenty.

King Pharoah come along behind
With all him army to make war
To take the Hebrews back for slaves again.
They come up close.
The Hebrews move out fast at night.
The soldiers come again.
The Hebrews move by day and night.
The soldiers come some more.
The Hebrews fear and run and then they reach a sea,
They reach a sea they no can cross.

They stop and cry.
    "How now?" they say.
    "How now?
    Moses done bring we here to die.

We no can swim
We no can find canoe
We no can ride a steamer.
How now?"

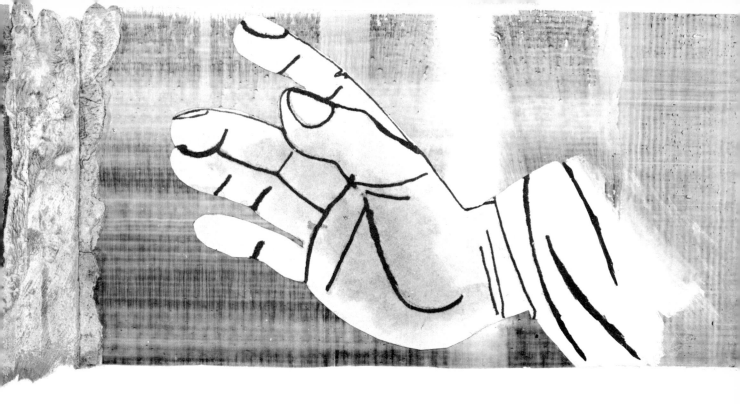

They cry and Moses self he fear
But Moses pray.
Now God can fix up anything.
God say
    "Moses, wait!
    I show who rule the land and water
    I show the people who can save them
    I show all people who the true God be.
    Wait!"
And Moses wait.

God say
    "Make the people meet Me on the beach!"
Moses do so.
God say
    "Moses,
    Hold out your stick,
    Hold it out over the water."
Moses do so.

Softly, softly east wind rise to blow.
It blow soft but with a force from God
And while the people look
They see the waters move.
Some water move one side and some the other
Some turn about and move and some move straight

Some move slow and some move quick
Some move in and some move out

Some come some go
But all do move.
While the people look
The waters open up and make a road down in the sea
While on two sides it rise and stand like mountains.
God say

"Go!
And while you go
I will go with you!"

The people fear to go
But Moses lead
And one man go behind
Then two, then three, then plenty more,
And all the people follow through
And no man wet him foot.

When Pharoah come he see the road
He see the Hebrews marching on.
He never see such thing before
He don't know God.
He say
    "I too will go
    And on the other side
    I take the Hebrew people.
    March!"
The army march.

They come on down the road
They no get wet till all the army march
With water high on one side and the other.
Then God reach down
And lay small trouble in the way
And men fall down and horses turn about.
The army stop.
The drummers beat they drums
The leaders call
The head men shout
The horn men blow they horns.
The king cry out.

Moses look down the road on the other side.
God speak softly to him.
Moses bow him head
He lift him stick
The waters go to move again
And water mountains fall and roll
And men cry out
While waves run high
And all the waters move about
Like they be vex.

And bye-m-bye a wave bring up King Pharoah dead

And lay him down
At Moses foot.

About the Author

Lorenz Graham was born in New Orleans, Louisiana, the son of a Methodist minister. He attended the University of California at Los Angeles for three years, then went to Africa to teach in a Liberian mission school.

Mr. Graham became interested in the tribal culture of his students and wanted to write about the African people. He returned to the United States and was graduated from Virginia Union University. Later he did postgraduate work at the New York School for Social Work and at New York University. He has worked with young people as a teacher and a social worker.

The author met his wife in Liberia, where she also was a teacher. They make their home in southern California and have traveled extensively in Africa and the Far East. Most of Mr. Graham's time is now given to writing.

About the Illustrator

Gregorio Prestopino's paintings have been exhibited at numerous museums, universities, and one-man shows throughout the United States. His work appears in many permanent collections, including those of the Whitney Museum and the Museum of Modern Art in New York City, the Chicago Art Institute, the Smithsonian Institution, and the National Institute of Arts and Letters.

Mr. Prestopino was born and educated in New York City. He has taught painting and drawing at the Museum of Modern Art, the Brooklyn Museum, and the New School. During 1968-1969, he served as painter-in-residence at the American Academy in Rome.

Mr. Prestopino finds particularly attractive in this story "the contemporary qualities . . . and the increasing battle between good and evil."